W9-BCR-404

# TECHNOLOGY IN TIMES PAST

# Ancient Egypt

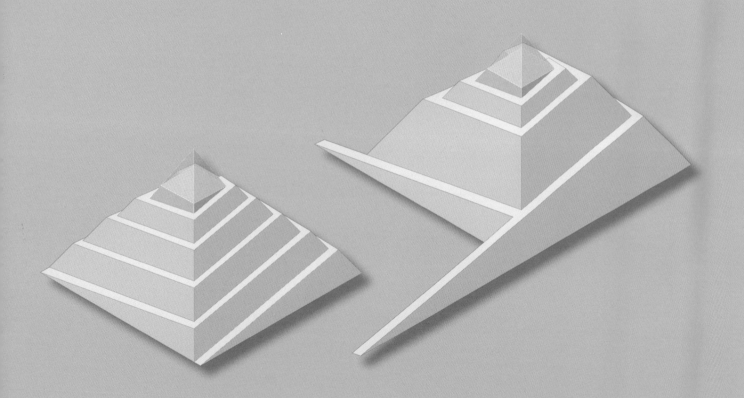

# ROBERT SNEDDEN

SAUNDERS
BOOK COMPANY

Published by Saunders Book Company
27 Stewart Road
Collingwood, ON Canada L9Y 4M7

Designed by Helen James
Edited by Pip Morgan
Illustrations by Graham Rosewarne
Picture research by Su Alexander

Library of Congress Cataloging-in-Publication Data

Snedden, Robert.
    Ancient Egypt / Robert Snedden.
    p. cm.–(Smart Apple Media–Technology in times past)
    Includes index.
    Summary: "Covers the inventions and technology used by Ancient Egyptians and how their ideas
    influenced technology today"–Provided by publisher.
    ISBN 978-1-897563-61-8 pbk
    1. Technology–Egypt–Juvenile literature. 2. Egypt–Civilization–To 332 B.C.–Juvenile literature. I.
Title.
T27.3.E3S645 2009
609.32–dc22

                                                                                        2007050933

Picture acknowledgements
Page 7t Bernard Annebicque/Corbis Sygma, b Yann Arthus-Bertrand/Corbis; 9 Musee du Louvre Paris/Gianni
Dagli Orti/The Art Archive; 10 Michael Nicholson/Corbis; 11 Lee Snider/Photo Images/Corbis; 12 Peter M.
Wilson/Corbis; 13 Tibor Bognar/Corbis; 14 Bettmann/Corbis; 15 Nathan Benn/Corbis; 16 Yann Arthus-Bertrand/
Corbis; 17t Erich Lessing/AKG Images, b Gilles Mermet/AKG Images; 18 Charles & Josette Lenars/Corbis; 19 The
Gallery Collection/Corbis; 20 & 21 Gianni Dagli Orti/Corbis; 22 Musee du Louvre Paris/Gianni Dagli Orti/The
Art Archive; 23 Erich Lessing/AKG Images; 24 Gianni Dagli Orti/Corbis; 25 Wolfgang Thieme/dpa/Corbis; 26
Minden Pictures/Getty Images; 27 Historical Picture Archive/Corbis; 28 Sandro Vannini/Corbis; 29 Trinette Reed/
Zefa/Corbis; 30 Gianni Dagli Orti/Corbis; 31 Brooklyn Museum/Corbis; 32 & 33t Staatliche Sammlung
Aygyptischer Kunst Munich/Gianni Dagli Orti/The Art Archive; 33b Egyptian MuseumTurin/Gianni Dagli Orti/
The Art Archive; 34 Egyptian Museum Cairo/Alfredo Dagli Orti/The Art Archive; 35 Bettmann/Corbis; 36 Robert
Holmes/Corbis; 37 Pharaonic Village Cairo/Gianni Dagli Orti/The Art Archive; 38 Alinari Archives/Corbis; 39t
Werner Forman/Corbis, b H.Benser/Zefa/Corbis; 40 The Art Archive/Corbis; 41 Stapleton Collection/Corbis:
Front cover Frans Lemmens/Zefa/Corbis

Printed in the United States of America
in North Mankato, Minnesota
052011
DAD0028c

9 8 7 6 5 4 3

# CONTENTS

# THE GIFT OF THE NILE

**For nearly 3,000 years, a great civilization flourished along the Nile River. The Greek traveler Herodotus, writing in about 450 B.C., called Egypt "the gift of the Nile." Most of Egypt is a desert, but people can live on the land on either side of the river. Each year, the waters of the Nile flood the land, leaving black silt that makes the soil fertile.**

## UPPER AND LOWER EGYPT

More than 5,000 years ago, the people who had settled along the valley of the Nile River united as a single kingdom, known as Upper Egypt. The people who lived around the river delta in the north belonged to another kingdom called Lower Egypt. These early Egyptians lived in houses of mud brick and knew how to use irrigation to take advantage of the Nile's annual flood. They also made tools and weapons from copper. Around 3100 B.C., the king of Upper Egypt conquered Lower Egypt and joined the two kingdoms.

In 2649 B.C., Egypt entered one of its greatest periods—a time known to historians as the Old Kingdom. During this period, the pyramids were built, the country of Egypt had a strong government, and its people made great progress in science and art.

## A REMARKABLE SOCIETY

There was nothing primitive about the ancient Egyptians. They were intelligent and well-organized people who created one of the world's first written languages. Their doctors were thought to be among the finest of the time. Their farmers managed the annual floods of the Nile with an irrigation system that ensured the most efficient use of water in their fields.

*This map shows the extent of the Egyptian empire in 1450 B.C.*

*The Great Pyramid and the Sphinx stand on the edge of the desert west of Cairo. Their stones have eroded over many centuries.*

The achievements of the ancient Egyptians would be hard to repeat today, even with modern technology. For example, we can only guess how they moved and erected the two million stone blocks (some weighing several tons) that form the Great Pyramid. The fact that today, 5,000 years later, people still stand and marvel at their great building feats is testimony to the genius of the Egyptians.

*An aerial view of the Nile River shows the fertile farmland that borders both of its banks.*

# Houses and Homes

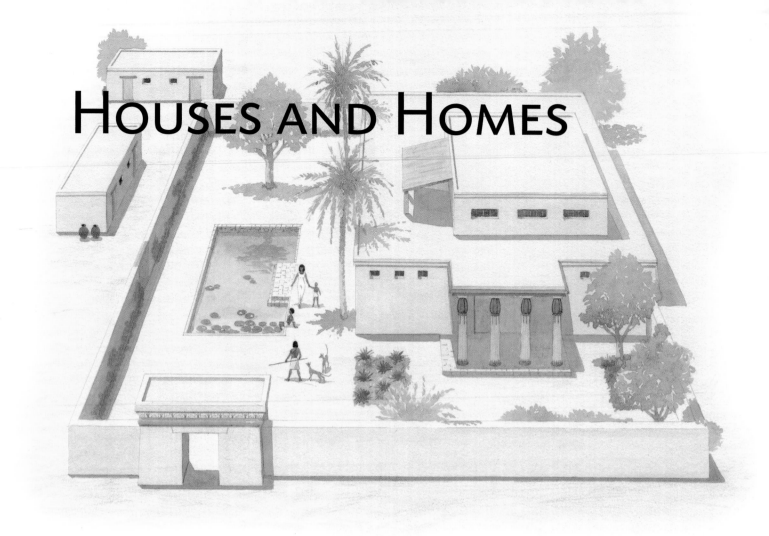

**There is little left of the homes the Egyptians lived in more than 5,000 years ago. They may have been made by weaving and binding the reeds that grew plentifully along the banks of the Nile River. By around 3800 B.C., houses built with sun-dried brick were common.**

*A nobleman's family might have lived in a townhouse such as this during the New Kingdom.*

## Brick Houses

The Egyptians made bricks for their houses by mixing mud from the bottom of the Nile with straw chaff. They placed the resulting mixture in wooden frames where it was shaped into bricks that were baked dry in the sun. A good brickmaker could produce more than 1,000 bricks in a day; this means that five days' work produced enough bricks to build a one-story house for a worker.

In the dry climate of Egypt, these mud bricks were good building materials. When the house was finished, the walls were covered with plaster to protect the bricks. Unless the house was affected by flooding, the walls would stand for many years.

A typical worker's house had between two and four rooms on the ground floor, an enclosed yard where food was prepared and cooked, and cellars for storage. An open staircase led to the flat roof, which the family used as additional living space. Here, they often cooked their food and slept during the summer to keep cool.

*These models of ancient Egyptian houses are made of a kind of baked clay called terra-cotta.*

## SANITATION

Some larger Egyptian homes had the luxury of bathrooms and toilets. Some of the toilet seats were made of limestone, while others had woven toilet stools, which had a hole in the seat and a bowl underneath. Families disposed of their household waste in pits, in the river, or in the streets. Drains made of copper pipe were sometimes used in temples, but never in private homes.

The Egyptians drew water from private or public wells. The largest public wells were about 16 feet (5 m) in diameter; a spiral staircase led down to the water. Sometimes

## PALM TREE WOOD

Ancient Egypt was a country with few trees (except palm trees), so the Egyptians had little wood to use for building houses. They made doors and window shutters out of palm tree wood. The upper floors were made of palm tree planks supported by wooden pillars. Wood was so precious that it was always reused whenever possible.

a shadoof raised the water from a well into a pond. Water from the Nile or canals caused health problems because of the parasites and other disease-causing organisms it contained.

# BUILDING IN STONE

**From around the time of the Old Kingdom, more than 4,500 years ago, the Egyptians began some massive building projects. They erected pyramids for their dead leaders, as well as temples and palaces. The fact that many of these have survived is proof of the skill of the Egyptian builders.**

The Egyptians had plenty of stone to build with—limestone, sandstone, and granite were all easily accessible. But extracting it, shaping it, and transporting it were difficult tasks (see pages 12–13). As a result, stone was only used for the most important buildings.

## GRAND TEMPLES

The Egyptians built many grand temples to their gods along the Nile River. Some of these temples are enormous. Usually, the front wall of a temple had two large sloping towers, together called a pylon. Between them, an

*The Temple of Amun in Karnak, near Luxor, was created around 1300 B.C. It is one of the grandest buildings in ancient Egypt.*

*Cleopatra's Needle in Central Park, New York, is an Egyptian obelisk that was made around 1500 B.C.*

entrance led to an open courtyard bordered by rows of evenly spaced stone columns. Beyond the courtyard stood the hypostyle hall, with a roof held high on sturdy pillars. Archaeologists believe that this grand hall represented a grove of trees.

At the heart of the building was the sanctuary of the temple god, a place only priests and the pharaoh were allowed to enter.

## OBELISKS

An obelisk is a square stone pillar with a pyramid shape on top. The Egyptians erected them in honor of the sun god, Re. Some obelisks weighed hundreds of tons so erecting them and making sure they were upright was no easy task. No one knows how they did this. They may have constructed a stone base

for the obelisk and then built a brick funnel around the base. Long ramps were extended to the top of the funnel, which was filled with sand.

The obelisk was dragged up the ramp, base first, to the mouth of the funnel. As sand was removed from the base of the funnel, the obelisk was gradually lowered into a standing position. Once the obelisk was in position, the ramps and funnel were taken down.

11

# PYRAMIDS

**Think of ancient Egypt and you almost certainly think of the pyramids. Without any of today's sophisticated tools and powerful equipment, the Egyptians built the ancient world's most amazing monuments.**

*Three pyramids rise up from the desert's edge at Giza. The Great Pyramid, built around 2600 B.C., is in the middle. For more than 4,000 years, it was the world's tallest building.*

## PLANNING AND PREPARATION

First, the Egyptians prepared the site where the pyramid was to be built. They removed the sand and gravel so that the pyramid could stand firmly on bare rock. Next, they leveled the area. To do this, they built an earth bank around the site and flooded it with water.

Engineers dug a series of channels in the rock, each at the same depth from the water surface. When the water was drained away, the spaces between the channels were dug down to the same level, giving a flat surface.

The Egyptians aligned the pyramids according to the stars. The master builder made careful observations to find the correct position for the base of the pyramid, which he then made into a perfect square. He used measuring cords made from flax fibers and a sighting tool called a bay, made from the central rib of a palm tree leaf.

Even though flax stretches, the cords were very accurate. For example, the Great Pyramid at Giza is about 755 feet (230 m) on each side, with only an 8-inch (20-cm) difference between

*The Egyptians may have built ramps to move the stones for the pyramids. One possibility is a long ramp to the top. Another ramp might have wound around the pyramid.*

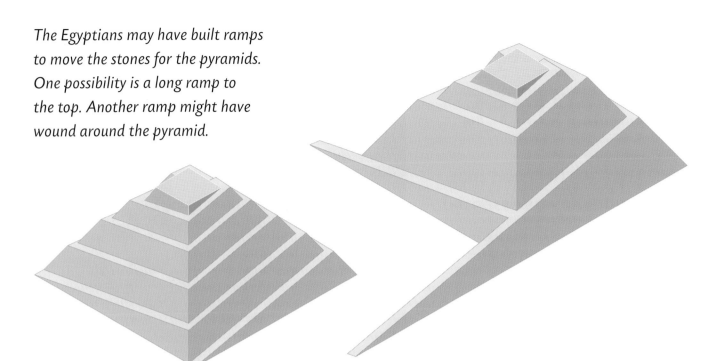

the longest and shortest sides. The ancient Egyptians aligned the sides of the Great Pyramid exactly north/south and east/west by taking very precise sightings of stars.

## Building Blocks

The huge limestone and granite blocks used to build the pyramids were cut from nearby quarries. Workers cut out the blocks with pickaxes, chisels, granite hammers, copper drills, and saws. Sometimes they split the rock by driving in wedges, then soaking them in water so that they expanded and cracked the rock.

Some of the stone blocks weighed as much as 55 tons (50 t). The easiest way to transport them to the building site was to take them as far as

possible by boat, then drag them on sleds along a causeway from the river.

The Egyptians had no lifting machinery, such as cranes, to raise the huge stone blocks into position. Instead, they constructed ramps (see above) that rose higher with the pyramid. Once the pyramid was finished, the ramps were removed.

*The glass pyramid in front of the main entrance to the Louvre in Paris shows how these structures still fascinate us.*

# PREPARING FOR THE AFTERLIFE

The Egyptians believed that a proper burial was essential if they wanted to live again in the afterlife. Ordinary Egyptians were probably wrapped in cloth and buried in the desert sand with a few personal items and a little food for the journey to the afterlife. Tombs for the wealthy had an underground chamber and an upper room with offerings for the gods. The pharaohs who ruled Egypt were buried in pyramids.

## MUMMIFICATION

The bodies of the wealthy were mummified before being buried. The Egyptians probably started to mummify bodies around 2600 B.C. First, the body was carefully washed. Next, a cut was made along the left-hand side of the body so that the internal organs, such as the stomach, liver, and lungs, could be removed. The heart was left because the Egyptians believed this was the organ of thought and the center of a person's being. The brain was pulled out through the nose with a long hook!

*The Pharoah Tutankhamen had three coffins. This gold coffin was the innermost of the three and contained the ruler's mummified body.*

The body was then embalmed. First, it was packed in a substance called natron to remove moisture. After 40 days, it was washed and rubbed with oils. The dried-up organs were wrapped in linen and put back into the body with other materials, such as sawdust and leaves, to give the body a more natural shape.

## WRAPPED UP

Fine strips of linen were wrapped around the body's head and around each of the fingers and toes. Then the rest of the body was wrapped. The arms were tied together, and so were the legs. More layers of linen bandages were added, covered with resin to help them stick together. Finally, a linen cloth was wrapped around the mummy and secured with strips of linen, around the middle and from top to bottom.

The mummy was lowered into a coffin, which was placed inside a second coffin. The double coffin was placed in a stone sarcophagus, which was laid inside the tomb. Food and drink, household objects, and valuables were put around the sarcophagus for the dead person to use in the afterlife.

Mummification preserved the body so well that we have a good idea of how ancient Egyptians looked when they were alive.

*This is the mummy of Ramses the Great who ruled Egypt from 1279 to 1213 B.C.*

## WEIGHING THE HEART

The Egyptians believed that the souls of the dead passed through seven gates and met Osiris, the god of the underworld. He judged them in a ritual known as "weighing the heart," which is why the heart is never removed during mummification.

# THE WATERS OF THE NILE

**The Egyptians were totally dependent on the Nile River for their water supply. Every year, beginning in June, the river flooded. It reached its peak in late September and then receded again. These floods deposited a fertile mud that enriched the soil around the river and ensured good harvests.**

## MEASURING THE WATER LEVEL

The water level of the Nile was crucial to the Egyptians, and they measured it using devices called nilometers. The simplest of these was a vertical column in the river, marked at regular intervals. In the 9th century A.D., a replica was made of an earlier nilometer. It stands 18 cubits high. A cubit is an ancient measurement that equals about one and a half feet (0.5 m). Other nilometers used a channel cut from the river and running into a tank or cistern. The higher the river, the fuller the tank. Knowing how much water there was allowed the Egyptians to calculate how much food they would be able to grow that season.

## IRRIGATING THE SOIL

The Egyptians managed their water with a system called basin irrigation. They built a series of banks of dirt, some along the river and some at right angles to it. These divided the land around the river into a series of flat valleys where people grew their crops. Wooden barriers could be opened or closed to direct the floodwaters into the valley and soak the soil. Excess water was drained off into another valley or a canal. Farmers planted their crops on the watered land.

*This nilometer measured the height of the water in the Nile.*

*Water from an irrigation canal flows into a field of crops after a farmer breaks a dam.*

The canals that bordered the valleys were separated from the river by dams. When the flood reached the mouth of the canals, the Egyptians opened the dams to let the water flow in and fill the canals. When the highest water level had been reached, the dams were rebuilt and the canals closed again to collect the water. The canals gave farmers a supply of water that they could channel into the fields.

## THE SHADOOF

Raising water up from the canals to higher land posed a problem. One solution, called a shadoof, had been invented in Mesopotamia (present-day Iraq) and was copied by the Egyptians. The shadoof is one of the simplest but most effective pieces of technology. It consists of a pole with a bucket at one end and a counterweight at the other. The pole is placed on a pivot and can be tipped up and down with ease. One man can raise more than 500 gallons (1,900 l) of water a day using a shadoof. You can see shadoofs working up and down the Nile today.

*A farmer uses a shadoof to raise water from an irrigation canal.*

# GROWING CROPS

**Egyptian farmers had to work hard to be sure of a good harvest. Their main crops were barley and various types of wheat. They also grew leafy salad crops, onions, and root vegetables, as well as pulses, such as lentils, beans, and chickpeas, and fruit, such as dates, figs, and grapes.**

## PLOWING

In most countries, farmers have to plow the soil before they can plant crops in it. Plowing breaks up the soil and helps to ensure that the roots of the growing plants can get enough nutrients. However, around the Nile, most of the nutrients are deposited on top of the soil by the river. An Egyptian farmer only needed a light plow to break up the soil so he could plant and cover up the seeds. These wooden plows were pulled by a couple of cows.

## SOWING

Egyptian farmers sowed their crops by walking over the field with a bag of seeds and scattering them across the land. Sometimes they used a plow to cover the seeds with a layer of soil. Occasionally, they drove sheep or other animals across the field to trample in the seeds.

*A painting of a man and his wife plowing their fields was found on the tomb of a workman called Sennedjem and dates back to the 13th century B.C.*

## Harvest Time

Every year, the harvest had to be gathered before the Nile River began to flood in June. Everyone helped to bring in the crops. Teams of reapers began harvesting in the south of the country and moved north as the crops ripened.

The reapers used wooden sickles shaped like the jaw of a donkey. Sharp flints were embedded like teeth in the sickle—iron sickles came into use at a later date. The reaper held the ears of corn in one hand and swept down with the sickle in the other hand to cut them free. The reaper left the ears of corn on the ground, and other workers, following behind, gathered them up into baskets.

*This wall painting of agricultural workers harvesting crops was found on a tomb that dates between 1550 and 1320 B.C.*

The gathered crop was taken for threshing, which separated the valuable grain from the rest of the plant, called the chaff. The crop was spread out on hard-packed soil, and cattle were driven over it, their hooves pressing out the grain. A winnowing fork was used to remove stalks, and wooden scoops tossed the grain and chaff into the air. The wind blew the light chaff away, while the heavier grain fell back to the ground where it could be collected. Some of the chaff and straw was kept for making mud bricks.

# IN THE KITCHEN

The kitchen in a typical Egyptian home was likely to be in the open air, either in a corner of the courtyard or perhaps on the flat roof of the house. Kitchen utensils included pots, pans, cups, and dishes made of clay. Food was cooked in earthen vessels (metal was too expensive for the average Egyptian) and served on pottery dishes. Wealthier people had dishes of faience, copper, or bronze.

## MAKING FIRE

The Egyptians usually made fires for cooking by rubbing two pieces of wood together. One piece was twirled between the palms so that it rubbed against the other, held firmly on the ground. The friction heated the soft, lower fire stick so that the kindling caught fire. Making fire was much easier with the invention of the bow drill. This wooden bow had a string wound tightly around a spike with a hollowed out drill cap made of stone or a nutshell on top (see page 21). The spike was pressed against the fire stick and rotated by moving the bow back and forth.

## MAKING BREAD

The Egyptians milled their grain into flour with a flat grinding stone called a saddle

The bow drill is a bow with a bowstring that is wrapped around the drill. Moving the bow like a saw turns the drill, which heats the fire stick.

## TOOTHACHE

The sieves the Egyptians used in making flour were made of rushes. They were not very efficient and let a lot of sand and flakes of stone fall through. The bread was gritty and wore down the Egyptians' teeth, so many of them suffered very badly from toothaches.

quern. At first, these grinding stones were placed on the floor, which made the milling process difficult. But in later years, the querns were raised on platforms, making the work a little less back-breaking.

Bread was made by mixing dough to which yeast, salt, spices, milk, and sometimes butter and eggs were added. The dough was either placed in pottery bread molds or shaped by hand. At first, it was cooked in open fires or even on the embers. Later, bakers used clay ovens that were big enough to bake several loaves at a time. Sometimes, the bakers slapped flat disks of dough onto the inner oven wall. They had to be sure to remove them when they were baked and before they fell off in to the embers.

*An Egyptian model (left) shows cooks working at various kitchen tasks—for example, making flour. The model is thought to date from the period known as the Middle Kingdom, between 2050–1786 B.C.*

*A papyrus whisk was found in the tomb of Kha, a royal architectural foreman, and his wife Meryt at Deir el-Medina, Egypt.*

# Metalworking

The Egyptians probably began to use metals for making things around 4000 B.C. They used copper first. Iron became popular around 900 B.C. The Egyptians made many things from copper, bronze, and iron, including tools, weapons, kitchen utensils, and jewelry.

## Copper

Copper ores were mined from the deserts between the Nile River and the Red Sea. Conditions for the miners were dreadful, and the work was usually done by slaves and convicted criminals.

The ores were smelted to extract the metal close to where they were mined. First, the ore was broken up into small pieces and mixed with charcoal in a shallow pit. The charcoal was then lit, producing temperatures that were high enough to separate the metal from the rock but not high enough to produce molten metal. The ashes left by the charcoal were raked off, and the copper was removed from the pit. Later, smelting operations became more sophisticated, using furnaces and bellows that could raise the temperature high enough to melt the copper.

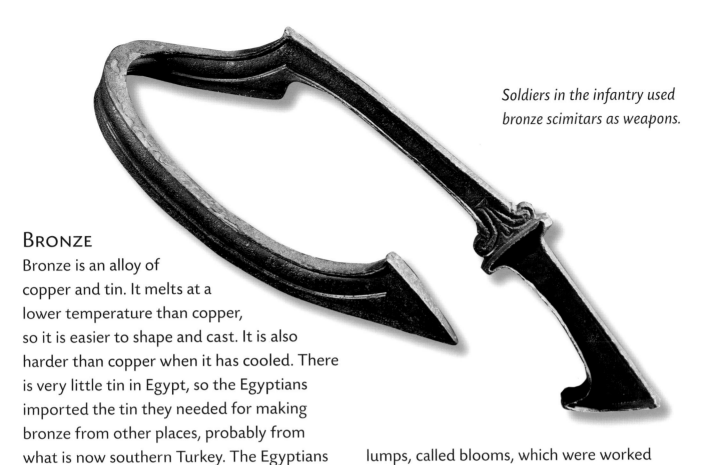

*Soldiers in the infantry used bronze scimitars as weapons.*

## BRONZE

Bronze is an alloy of copper and tin. It melts at a lower temperature than copper, so it is easier to shape and cast. It is also harder than copper when it has cooled. There is very little tin in Egypt, so the Egyptians imported the tin they needed for making bronze from other places, probably from what is now southern Turkey. The Egyptians made many things from bronze, ranging from temple doors and pots and pans to rings, tools, and weapons, such as arrowheads, spears, and battle-axes.

## IRON

Much higher temperatures are needed to smelt iron than the Egyptians could achieve in their furnaces. The iron was produced as solid lumps, called blooms, which were worked on forges while hot to form bars of wrought iron. The Egyptians knew how to make steel by adding a small amount of carbon to the iron. Unlike bronze or iron, steel can be made harder by quenching it, which involves rapidly cooling the hot metal by plunging it into cold water. Quenching also makes the steel brittle, so then it is reheated to a lower temperature to make it tougher. This is called tempering.

*The Egyptians used a copper bowl and water carrier called an ewer (left) for washing themselves.*

## METAL OF HEAVEN

**The Egyptians called iron "the metal of heaven." This was because the first iron they had came from iron-rich meteorites that fell to the desert from space. The oldest-known iron objects, found at two sites on the banks of the Nile, are beads that are around 6,000 years old. Analysis of the iron showed that it came from meteorites.**

# CARPENTRY

**The only trees that grew in Egypt were mostly of low quality wood, such as palm trees. Better quality woods, such as pine and cedar, were imported from Lebanon and eastern Africa. There was always plenty of work for Egyptian carpenters.**

### AXES AND SAWS

Egyptian carpenters worked in groups rather than alone, and they used tools that would be familiar to a carpenter today. The main tool for splitting wood into planks was the ax. Saws were used for cutting wood, but they were very hard to use. An Egyptian saw was a pull saw, cutting only when it was pulled, not pushed, through the wood. Saws were made from copper, which is too soft, and bronze, which is too brittle to make good saw teeth.

### ADZES AND CHISELS

Planing and carving were done with an adze. The adze was a blade attached to a wooden handle. Early Egyptians used blades made

# THE FIRST MACHINE TOOL

The ancient Egyptians developed the world's first machine tool, a lathe, about 2,500 years ago. Lathes make it easy for people to produce rounded objects, such as a bowl and a chair leg. The wood is turned like a bow drill by means of a cord wrapped around it. One man pulled the bow back and forth to make the wood spin, while another shaped it with a chisel.

*A student uses a modern lathe at a school for making wooden toys.*

of stone, such as obsidian, which is a black volcanic glass that can be ground into a very sharp edge. A carpenter had a number of adzes of different sizes and used large ones for cutting house timbers and smaller ones for more delicate work.

An Egyptian carpenter also had a range of chisels with different-sized blades to suit a range of tasks. He used the smallest blades for detailed carving. The handles of the chisels were rounded to fit comfortably into the

*This model (left) of a carpentry workshop was made around 2000 B.C. It shows one carpenter using a saw while others work with adzes.*

carpenter's hand. He struck the handle with a wooden mallet when carving wood.

## DRILLS

The Egyptians made holes in wood with a bow drill (see page 21). The first drills were sticks with pointed stones attached to one end. Rotating the stick between the palms of the hands turned the drill. The bow drill, which had the string of a bow wound around the drill stick, was much more effective.

Carpenters joined two pieces of wood using wooden dowels. These wooden pins are pressed into holes drilled into the pieces of wood they wanted to join together.

25

# Papyrus

**Papyrus is a reed that grows along the banks of the Nile. The Egyptians wove its fibers to make baskets, sandals, ropes, and boats. They made mattresses for their beds as well as medicine and perfumes. They even ate the roots. But perhaps the best-known use was for making paper.**

*Papyrus reeds grow in the freshwater marshes of the Nile. The reeds can grow nearly ten feet (3 m) tall.*

## PAPERMAKING

After harvesting the plants, the Egyptians peeled away the outer fibers of the stalk. The core of the stalk was sliced into very thin, broad strips. Strips from the center of the stalk gave the best quality paper. The strips were soaked in water to remove sugar (the Egyptians enjoyed chewing papyrus roots for their sweetness) and then pounded. A row of the soaked strips were placed side by side on a linen board, overlapping slightly. A second set of strips was laid over the top at right angles to the first set, again overlapping slightly.

The overlapping strips of papyrus were then covered with another sheet of linen and pounded again before being pressed under a heavy weight, such as a stone slab, and left to dry. After drying, the sheet of paper was carefully peeled away from the linen and polished to a smooth finish by rubbing with a shell or a piece of smooth ivory.

Papyrus was made in different qualities, just as we have different qualities of paper today. The quality depended on the age of the plants, where they were harvested, and the

*Making paper from papyrus involved several stages: slicing the stalks into strips; soaking the*

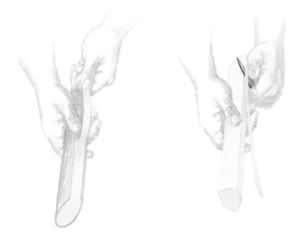

*strips in water; laying the strips on a linen board; pounding and pressing the overlapping strips; drying the sheet; and polishing the paper.*

part of the stalk used. Merchants wrapped their goods in very coarse cheap paper. The finest paper was kept for religious writings and other important records.

## WRITING

The invention of writing was enormously important in the advance of technology and civilization. It meant that accurate records were kept and knowledge was passed on from one person to another. No one is certain when people first began to keep written records. There is evidence that the people of

Mesopotamia (present-day Iraq) developed a form of writing about 5,000 years ago and that the Egyptians followed a couple of hundred years later. Around 2000 B.C., the Egyptians invented the world's first alphabet.

## READING PICTURES

The Egyptians had three writing systems. One used hieroglyphs, which are pictures of objects. Each picture corresponded to the sound of one or more letters. Hieroglyphs were not a series of pictures like a cartoon, but a language that was read.

*A scene from the Judgement of the Dead, painted on papyrus. There are columns of hieroglyphs in the background.*

27

# Textiles and Clothing

Most of the clothes the Egyptians wore were made from linen. Linen is made from flax, a plant that the Egyptians grew beside their grain crops. The Egyptian weavers were skillful and produced delicate cloth. The very best quality cloth was kept for people of high rank or great wealth.

### Preparing Fibers

When the flax plants were ready to be harvested, they were pulled up in bundles, rather than cut. The bundles of flax fibers were soaked in water, which started to break down the tough outer parts of the plant. After a time, the soaked plants were beaten using wooden mallets and then combed out to remove the flax fibers.

### Spinning and Weaving

In the next stage, the fibers were spun into thread, or yarn, using a hand spindle. This was a weighted stick that the spinner set spinning on the ground. The spinner teased out fibers from the flax and allowed them to twist around the spindle to make the thread. Once the fibers had been spun into thread, they were ready for weaving.

The Egyptians were weaving cloth 7,000 years ago. The first weavers used a simple horizontal, or ground, loom. They made this

*Many ancient Egyptian paintings show the kind of clothes that people wore.*

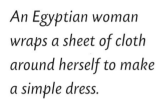

*An Egyptian woman wraps a sheet of cloth around herself to make a simple dress.*

by hammering four pegs into the ground to form a rectangular frame. Two crossbars were fitted across the frame to hold the threads. The weaver had to crouch on the ground to weave the cloth.

From about 1500 B.C., the Egyptians began to use upright vertical looms mounted on heavy wooden frames. These took up less space and were used indoors, but it took more physical effort to operate them.

## WHAT PEOPLE WORE

The clothes, which were mostly made by women, were very simple and required very little sewing. Men wore a short loincloth and women wore a dress with straps. Both sexes also wore a robe called a *kalasiris*. These were

sewn from a rectangular piece of cloth with a hole cut in the middle for the wearer's head to go through. The sides were stitched together and holes left for the arms. These clothes did not change much throughout Egypt's long history.

## WIGS

The Egyptians were very concerned with the way their hair looked. They often had elaborate hairstyles whether they were rich or poor. Both men and women shaved off their hair and wore wigs made of human hair padded with vegetable fibers beneath. These wigs were often woven into a complex arrangement of braids and strands.

*Modern wigs are made from artificial materials as well as from human hair.*

# POTTERY

Pottery is the craft of making things from clay and is one of our most important inventions. Pots are easy to make in practically any shape or size. They can be put to a wide variety of uses, such as storing food and protecting it from rats and mice.

## SHAPING CLAY

The oldest pots were either shaped by hand from a single lump of clay or they were built up by laying coils of clay on top of one another. From around 3000 B.C., Egyptian potters made plates and bowls by molding the clay around shaped pieces of wood.

A few centuries later, the potter's wheel was used in Egypt for the first time. The

*These pots were used for holding ointments. They were made from alabaster around 1500 B.C.*

potter's wheel may have been invented in Mesopotamia, but no one is certain. The earliest versions were turntables rotated by hand. They didn't change the way pots were made, but they allowed the potter to see his work from all sides more easily. The fast-spinning kick wheel, which is used by potters today, was invented 2,000 years later.

## FIRING THE CLAY

The earliest clay pots were left to dry in the sun. But sun-dried clay is not watertight, so its uses were limited. To make a pot watertight, it must be fired at a high temperature in a kiln. The kiln was probably invented in Asia. The Chinese had kilns around 6,500 years ago. By about 5,000 years ago, they were also being used in Egypt.

The kilns the Egyptians used had a lower chamber that held the fire. A chimney connected this to an open-topped upper chamber where the pots were placed for firing. Then the top of the chamber was sealed with clay to keep the heat in.

## FAIENCE

The Egyptians were masters of the art of making jewelry and other decorative objects from faience (pronounced *fay-ance*). Like clay, faience is a type of ceramic. It is made from crushed quartz or sand with small amounts of lime and ash added.

Water was added to the mixture to make a paste that could be shaped. Before the faience was fired to harden it, the Egyptians added a glaze, which was usually a blue-green color.

## THOUSANDS OF TILES
The step pyramid at Saqqara was the first pyramid in Egypt. It was built as the burial place of King Djoser around 2630 B.C. The underground chambers were decorated with approximately 36,000 blue-green faience tiles.

*This blue-green monkey is a figurine made of faience around 1350 B.C.*

# GLASSMAKING

## THE RIGHT TEMPERATURE

The secret of glassmaking may have come from making faience. Both glass and faience are mostly made of silica, the main constituent of sand.

The glass we use today is made from pure silica, but this needs a temperature of more than 3,000°F (1,650°C) to melt it—far too high for the ancient Egyptians to achieve. Adding a little alkali (such as soda or potash) to the silica lowers its melting point.

The ingredients for the glass were first ground up as finely as possible and mixed together. Next, the mixture was heated to around 1,400°F (760°C). The molten mixture was stirred more or less continuously for several hours to get air out of it.

*Three loops were molded onto this blue glass bowl so that it could be suspended from above. The bowl was made during the 18th Dynasty (1539–1292 B.C.).*

The mixture, called a frit, was allowed to cool and harden. Then it was ground up into a powder again. Finally, it was reheated at a higher temperature than before—perhaps around 2,000°F (1,100°C)—and poured into molds. The glassmakers had no protection from the fierce heat.

32

## GLASSBLOWING

The Egyptians had all they needed to practice glassblowing, but it seems they never brought together all of the different elements. The pipes they used to blow air into the furnaces could have been adapted for blowing glass; they could reach the temperatures needed to make the glass molten; and they were skilled at glass manufacture. In fact, glassblowing didn't come to Egypt until the Romans conquered it during the 1st century B.C.

## SHAPING THE GLASS

The Egyptians developed a clever way of shaping glass. A clay shape was formed and attached to the end of a metal rod. The glass-maker built up layers of glass over the clay, sometimes using different colors of glass to make a pleasing design. The glass was rolled on a stone slab to make it smooth on the outside. Once the glass had cooled, the clay core was removed.

*Thutmose III, who was Pharoah of Egypt between 1479 and 1425 B.C., owned this blue glass drinking vessel.*

*These pieces of glassware were made during the New Kingdom.*

Another way of shaping glass was to take a large block of it and carve it like a block of stone. Glass is very brittle and liable to shatter, so this took a great deal of skill and was only rarely attempted.

33

# Traveling by Water

**The Nile was the Egyptians' main transportation link, as it flowed from one end of the country to the other. From the earliest days of the kingdom, the Egyptians took to the river in boats: for fishing, for moving goods from place to place, and for pleasure.**

### Papyrus Boats

The Egyptians lacked a good source of wood, so they looked for other materials to make boats. Once again, they turned to the useful papyrus. The first boats were rafts made of papyrus reeds bundled together. They were cheap and easy to make. Gradually, the Egyptians developed larger ships with sickle-shaped hulls that enabled them to take to the sea. Some of these reed-ships were equipped with masts and deckhouses to house the crew.

When traveling south, or upstream on the Nile, sails propelled the boats along. On the way north, or downstream, the current of the river carried the boats and the masts were taken down.

### Wooden Ships

Reed boats weren't strong enough for heavier duties such as transporting large cargos. For these purposes, the Egyptians built wooden ships

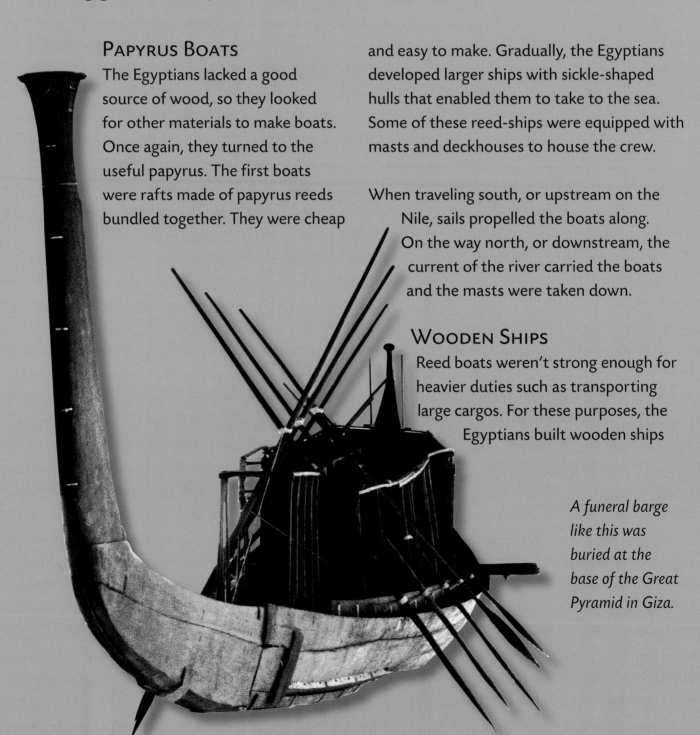

*A funeral barge like this was buried at the base of the Great Pyramid in Giza.*

*Norwegian explorer Thor Heyerdahl built this papyrus boat and tried to cross the Atlantic Ocean in it in 1969.*

from acacia or cedar wood. During the second millennium B.C., obelisks weighing 330 tons (300 t) were transported down river from Aswan in specially reinforced ships.

Carpenters built the ships in shipyards. They took just over two weeks to build a 98-foot (30-m) long barge for carrying cargo. Ships were built without nails or pegs. Instead, the planks of wood were fastened together with papyrus ropes. The wooden ships were flat-bottomed with square sterns and were similar to the reed boats. The ship's mast was often two-legged and attached to the gunwale (the upper edge of the boat's sides). The sails on Egyptian ships were always square. Steering a ship was hard work. Helmsmen held two large oars in both hands. Later, the oars were connected to a tiller.

## THE PHAROS LIGHTHOUSE

Around 270 B.C., the Egyptians built the Pharos lighthouse at Alexandria where the Nile flows into the Mediterranean Sea. Alexandria was one of the most important ports in the Mediterranean. The lighthouse was more than 300 feet (100 m) high and was visible from about 30 miles (48 km). During the day, a large mirror was used to reflect the sun out to sea to show the sailors on incoming ships where the harbor was, and at night, a fire was lit.

## FIGUREHEADS

Sometimes the Egyptians attached a figurehead to the bow of a ship. Egyptian figureheads looked back toward the deck of the ship, unlike those on later European ships, which faced forward to the open sea.

35

# TIMEKEEPING

**Keeping track of time was important to the Egyptians. For example, knowing when the Nile floods would come was vitally important. If the Egyptians weren't ready for the water, they risked a failed harvest and starvation.**

## FIRST DATE

The Egyptians realized that the star Sirius, which they called Sopdet, rose in a direct line with the rising sun once every 365 days. This was about the same time as the annual flood of the Nile began. They devised a 365-day calendar that began on the first date recorded in human history—4241 B.C. The astronomers showed that the year was really 365 and a quarter days long.

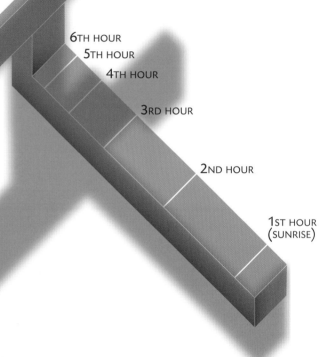

6TH HOUR
5TH HOUR
4TH HOUR
3RD HOUR
2ND HOUR
1ST HOUR
(SUNRISE)

*A shadow clock tracks the shadow of the sun in the first six hours after sunrise.*

*A modern sundial at the Joe Brown Memorial Park in New Orleans, Louisiana.*

## SHADOW CLOCKS

The Egyptians were one of the first people to divide the day into different parts, just as we divide it into hours. The shadows of their obelisks moved around as the sun moved across the sky. Noon was when the shadow was shortest. The longest and shortest days of the year were when the shadow at noon was shortest and longest respectively. Sundials, the first portable timekeepers, came in around 1500 B.C. The markings on the face of the sundial divided the day into ten daylight hours and two twilight hours.

## WATER CLOCKS

Water clocks were among the earliest mechanical timepieces that told the time without relying on the movement of heavenly bodies, such as the sun and stars. Some took the form of stone vessels with sloping sides that allowed water to drip out from a small hole near the bottom. Others were cylindrical or bowl-shaped containers designed to fill up as water dripped in at a constant rate.

Markings on the inside of the containers measured the passage of time as the water level rose or fell depending on the type of water clock.

Another version, which is still used in North Africa today, consisted of a metal bowl with a hole in the bottom. When it was placed in a container of water the bowl filled up and sank in a specific amount of time.

Water clocks were used to mark the passage of time at night, but they could just as well have been used in daylight. One of the earliest examples of a water clock was found in the tomb of the pharaoh Amenhotep I, who was buried around 1500 B.C. The Greeks, who began using them about 325 B.C., named them *clepsydras*, or "water thieves."

*A water clock is filled with water. It then empties at a fixed rate through the vertical rows of small and evenly-spaced holes in the sides.*

# Magic and Medicine

**The causes of illness were a mystery to the Egyptians, and they believed that evil spirits or the gods were responsible. However, the Egyptians knew a great deal about diseases and were good medical practitioners. They knew how to set bones, perform surgery, and use a variety of herbal remedies.**

## Surgery

Life for the Egyptians was physically hard and injuries were common. Egyptian doctors treated broken limbs with techniques very similar to those used by doctors today.

First, they lined up the broken bone properly. Then, they set it in either a wooden splint wrapped in bandages or encased in a plaster cast. This cast was made from milk mixed with barley or acacia leaves and bound together using gum and water.

If a limb was very badly damaged, the doctor might amputate it. The Egyptians may have made artificial limbs to help people who had suffered amputation. False arms and feet have been found with mummies, but we don't know if these were used in life, or provided after death for use in the afterlife.

The practice of mummification (see page 14), which involved removing most of the internal organs, gave the Egyptians some idea of what was inside the human body. They had a good knowledge of anatomy and an understanding of what each organ did, although they believed that thinking took place in the heart rather than the brain.

*A statue of Sekhmet, the Egyptian goddess of war, who is shown as a lioness. She was also the goddess of doctors and surgeons.*

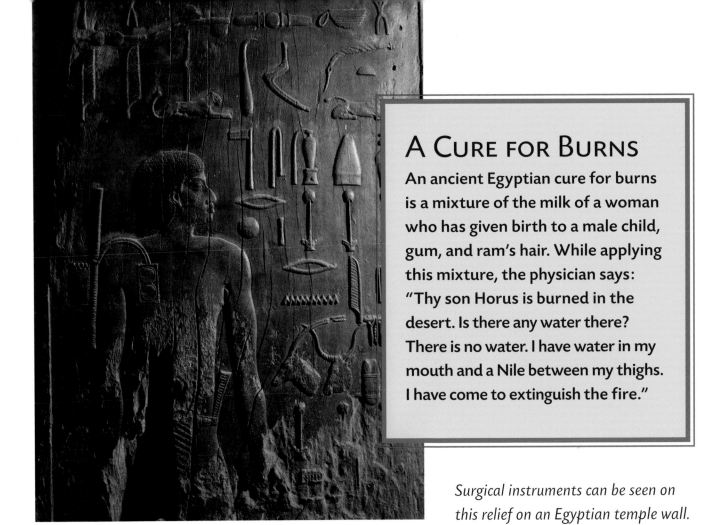

## A Cure for Burns

An ancient Egyptian cure for burns is a mixture of the milk of a woman who has given birth to a male child, gum, and ram's hair. While applying this mixture, the physician says: "Thy son Horus is burned in the desert. Is there any water there? There is no water. I have water in my mouth and a Nile between my thighs. I have come to extinguish the fire."

*Surgical instruments can be seen on this relief on an Egyptian temple wall.*

## Dentistry

The gritty flour the Egyptians made into bread wore down their teeth badly (see page 21). We know there were dentists in Egypt from around 2650 B.C. They could do little to cure dental problems and were more concerned with preventing them, if they could.

Swollen gums were treated with a mixture of cumin, incense, and onion. Sometimes holes were drilled into the jawbone to drain abscesses, but as far as we know, they did not pull out teeth.

## Priest-doctors

The Egyptian priest-doctors first had to discover the nature of the evil spirit possessing the person before they could find a way to drive it out. This was done by means of magic rituals, spells, and talismans. Medicines in the form of herbs might be used to ease the sufferer's pain, but any cure that came about was a result of the magic.

*Modern plaster casts are made from plaster of Paris, but are quite similar to casts used in ancient Egypt.*

# MILITARY TECHNOLOGY

Egyptian soldiers were equipped with various weapons. In the early days, they had throwing sticks, spears, slingshots, cudgels, maces, daggers, and battle-axes. Later, bows and arrows, body armor and chariots joined the soldier's arsenal.

*Models of archers in the Egyptian army from the 11th Dynasty, around 2000 B.C.*

## BOW AND ARROW

The main weapon of the Egyptians was the bow and arrow. Early bows were made of wood, with strings of plant fiber or animal sinews. Later came the composite bow, which was made of wood, horn, and sinew. The bow curved forward when unstrung, so stringing it involved bending it back. This put extra tension on the bow and enabled the archer to shoot farther, but it also made stringing more difficult. Egyptian arrowheads were first made of flint, then copper was used around 2000 B.C.

## THE CHARIOT

The war chariot was probably invented in Syria and came to Egypt with the Hyksos army (see page 43) when it invaded around 1650 B.C. The Egyptians were quick to see the advantage of a fast-moving mobile fighting unit. They soon had chariots of their own, and then they drove the Hyksos from their country.

The Syrian chariot was a heavy vehicle, so the Egyptians improved its design. They made the frame and wheels lighter so that it could move faster. The two-man crew, a driver and an archer, stood in a semi-circular wooden housing that was open at the back. The wood for the housing was immersed in very hot water for several hours, then bent into shape and allowed to dry.

To make the spokes for the wheels, chariot makers bent strips of wood into "V" shapes,

## WARSHIPS

The Egyptians built warships from bundles of reeds tied together and coated with pitch to waterproof them. A warship had a narrow, sharp-ended hull and was fitted with a two-legged mast and a large square sail. More than 20 oarsmen on each side of the ship sped it through the water. Archers and spearmen attacked the enemy from raised decks. Some warships were fitted with a ram for battering enemy ships.

then glued them together. The wheel rims were sections of wood attached to the spokes with strips of leather.

*Ramesses II stands in his war chariot with his bow and arrow ready. The scene shows the Battle of Kadesh in Syria in 1279 B.C.*

# EGYPTIAN TIME LINE

Historians divide the history of Egypt into a number of different periods. These are:

The Predynastic Period ca. 5000–3100 B.C.

The Archaic Period ca. 3100–2649 B.C.

The Old Kingdom ca. 2649–2150 B.C.

The First Intermediate Period ca. 2150–2040 B.C.

The Middle Kingdom ca. 2040–1640 B.C.

The Second Intermediate Period ca. 1640–1552 B.C.

The New Kingdom ca. 1552–1069 B.C.

The Third Intermediate Period ca. 1069–664 B.C.

The Late Period ca. 664–332 B.C.

The Ptolemies ca. 332–30 B.C.


**ca. 7000 B.C.** The first people begin to settle in the Nile Valley.

**4241 B.C.** The Egyptians begin the first calendar.

**ca. 3700 B.C.** Copper, gold, and silver are smelted in furnaces.

**ca. 3500 B.C.** Cattle-drawn plows are used; barley and wheat are grown. Papyrus is made from papyrus reeds.

**ca. 3100 B.C.** Egypt becomes a united country when Menes, King of Upper Egypt, conquers Lower Egypt.

**ca. 2650 B.C.** The Egyptians adopt a 365-day calendar.

**ca. 2649–2150 B.C.** The pyramids are built during this period. The first step pyramid (the first Egyptian building made entirely of stone) is built for King Djoser.

**ca. 2600 B.C.** Egyptian doctors use splints to set broken arms. Egyptians begin to use bronze.

**ca. 2590 B.C.** The Great Pyramid of Giza—the Pyramid of Khufu—is built.

**ca. 2550 B.C.** The Great Sphinx at Giza is carved.

**ca. 2500 B.C.** The Egyptians begin to mummify their dead before burial. A system of canals and sluices controls distribution of the Nile's water.

**ca. 2050 B.C.** Domesticated cats are introduced to Egypt.

**ca. 2000 B.C.** Ovens for baking bread come into use.

**ca. 1674 B.C.** The Hyksos people from the Middle East attack and conquer Egypt. The horse and chariot, and the compound bow of horn and wood, are introduced to Egypt by the Hyksos.

**ca. 1580 B.C.** The Hyksos are driven from Egypt by Ahmose I.

**ca. 1555 B.C.** The shadoof comes into use along the Nile.

**1552–1069 B.C.** The Egyptian empire is at its strongest —royal tombs are built in the Valley of the Kings.

**ca. 1500 B.C.** Vertical looms are used for weaving.

**1490–1436 B.C.** The reign of Pharaoh Tuthmosis II, the greatest of the warrior pharaohs.

**ca. 1490 B.C.** Glass vessels are produced; bronze saws are in use.

**ca. 1450 B.C.** Bellows replace blowpipes in furnaces.

**ca. 1230 B.C.** A canal is dug connecting the Nile to the Red Sea.

**ca. 1200 B.C.** The beginning of the Iron Age—iron slowly begins to replace bronze. The Egyptians build ships more than 195 feet (59 m)long and make expeditions to the Indian Ocean.

**ca. 600 B.C.** An expedition sails around the continent of Africa.

**529 B.C.** Egypt is conquered by the Persians.

**405 B.C.** Egypt regains its independence from the Persians.

**343 B.C.** The Persians reconquer Egypt.

**332 B.C.** Alexander the Great occupies Egypt.

**286 B.C.** The great library of Alexandria is founded.

**280 B.C.** The Pharos lighthouse is constructed.

**197 B.C.** A decree by Ptolemy V is inscribed on a stone in Greek and in two forms of Egyptian, one of which is hieroglyphics. (The discovery of the Rosetta Stone in 1799 allowed modern-day researchers to decipher hieroglyphics for the first time in 1822.)

**47 B.C.** The destruction of the library at Alexandria; more than half a million books are lost in the fire.

**30 B.C.** Egypt becomes a Roman province.

# GLOSSARY

**acacia** A type of spiny tree or shrub.

**alabaster** Marble-like stone.

**alkali** A substance that combines with an acid to form salts.

**alloy** A mixture of two or more different metals; for example, bronze is an alloy formed by mixing copper and tin.

**amputation** Surgery to remove all or part of a limb, or another external part of the body.

**anatomy** The study of the structure of living things.

**bay** A sighting tool used by Egyptian surveyors to help them lay out straight lines.

**causeway** A raised roadway for crossing marshy or swampy ground.

**ceramic** An object made from clay and hardened by firing.

**chaff** Seed coverings and other inedible parts of a plant that are separated from the grain.

**cumin** Spice from a plant that was once native to the Nile Valley but is now grown all over the world.

**dowel** A wooden pin used to join two pieces of wood together; the dowel fits into holes drilled in each piece.

**embalming** A process for preserving human remains after death.

**faience** A type of glazed earthenware, usually a greenish-blue color.

**flax** A type of plant cultivated for its seeds and the fibers from its stem, which can be woven into cloth.

**flint** A type of hard stone.

**hieroglyph** A picture symbol in the Egyptian system of writing.

**hypostyle** A building in which the ceiling is supported by rows of columns.

**incense** A substance that produces a pleasing scent when it is burned.

**irrigation** A system of watering crops.

**lathe** A tool used to shape wood by spinning it at high speed while it is cut using chisels.

**loincloth** Material wrapped around the hips to cover the lower part of the body.

**Mesopotamia** The land between the Tigris and Euphrates rivers in what is now southern Iraq; the name means "between the rivers."

**mummification** The process of preserving the bodies of the dead.

**natron** A mixture of salts such as sodium carbonate and sodium bicarbonate.

**nilometer** A device for measuring the level of water in the Nile River.

**obelisk** A slim, four-sided pillar of stone ending in a pyramid shape at the top.

**ore** Rock from which metals can be obtained.

**papyrus** A type of reed and the paper from which it is made.

**parasite** An organism that lives in or on the tissues of another organism.

**pharaoh** A ruler of ancient Egypt.

**pylon** A large sloping wall at the entrance to a temple; pylon means "gate" in Greek.

**quartz** A hard, shiny mineral formed from crystals of silicon dioxide; found in most rocks, especially granite and sandstone.

**resin**  A clear sticky substance produced by some plants and used for making adhesives.

**sanitation**  Keeping clean and hygienic conditions, especially to prevent the spread of disease.

**sarcophagus**  A decorated stone container which held the coffin containing a mummy.

**shadoof**  A bucket and lever device for raising water from one level to another.

**sickle**  A short-handled tool with a sharp curved blade for harvesting crops by hand.

**sighting tool**  A tool for lining up one object with another some distance away.

**sinew**  The tissue that connects muscle to bone, also called tendons.

**smelting**  The process of heating and melting ores to extract the metals they contain.

**talisman**  A piece of jewelry thought to protect the wearer from harm.

**temper**  To toughen metal by heating it to a temperature below its melting point and then cooling it slowly.

**wrought iron**  Iron that has been worked by hammering.

# FURTHER READING

**Gogerly, Liz**. *Ancient Egypt. Time Travel Guides.* Chicago: Raintree, 2007.

**Hewitt, Sally**. *The Egyptians. Starting History.* North Mankato, Minn.: Smart Apple Media, 2007.

**MacDonald, Fiona.** *The Ancient Egyptians. Hands-on History.* North Mankato, Minn.: QEB Pub., 2007.

**Solodky, M**. *The Technology of Ancient Egypt.* New York: Rosen Pub. Group, 2006.

# WEB SITES

**Web Sites for Kids:**
**http://www.egyptvoyager.com/virtualtours.htm**
Take a virtual tour of the pyramids of Giza and six other exciting destinations in Egypt.

**http://www.rom.on.ca/schools/egypt/learn**
Learn more about the ancient Egyptians' everyday life at this site by the Royal Ontario Museum.

**Web Sites for Teachers:**
**http://www.timeforkids.com/TFK/teachers/aw/wr/main/0,28132,535892,00.html**
Teach students the Egyptian language and then take them on a tour of Egypt with helpful worksheets.

**http://school.discoveryeducation.com/lessonplans/programs/wheelofpharaoh/**
This site is filled with activity ideas for students learning about ancient Egypt, including the game "Wheel of Pharaoh."

# INDEX